Shade of Blue Trees

Shade of Blue Trees

{poems}

Dear Loretta —
with gratitude for reading
my book — may there be
lines that resonate with
you — with warmest
wishes,

Kelly
9/23/21

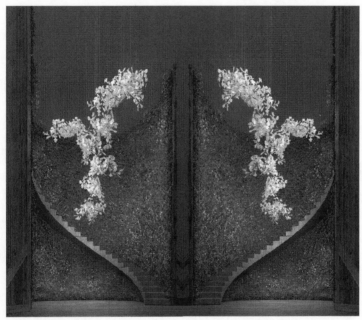

Kelly Cressio-Moeller

Kelly Cressio-Moeller

Finalist for the Two Sylvias Press Wilder Prize

Two Sylvias Press

Two Sylvias Press
PO Box 1524
Kingston, WA 98346
twosylviaspress@gmail.com

Cover Artist: Andreea Braescu, "Gingko Porcelain Light Sculpture"
Cover Design: Kelli Russell Agodon
Book Design: Annette Spaulding-Convy
Author Photo: Stefan Moeller

Created with the belief that great writing is good for the world, Two Sylvias Press mixes modern technology, classic style, and literary intellect with an eco-friendly heart. We draw our inspiration from the poetic literary talent of Sylvia Plath and the editorial business sense of Sylvia Beach. We are an independent press dedicated to publishing the exceptional voices of writers.

For more information about Two Sylvias Press please visit:
www.twosylviaspress.com

First Edition. Created in the United States of America.

ISBN: 978-1-948767-14-9

Two Sylvias Press
www.twosylviaspress.com

Praise for *Shade of Blue Trees*

The poems of Kelly Cressio-Moeller's *Shade of Blue Trees* offer up an intimate surrealism, earth-born, deeply shaded, and tinted the deep blue of solitude, memory, and myth, turning "yearning's blue fire into a / dreamscape fugue." Nowhere is Cressio-Moeller's virtuosity more apparent than in the sequence of "panels." These pieces function as lyric poems, language-paintings, fairy tales, and compressed novels, somehow removed from time, with a lushness that reminds me of Flaubert—without the meanness. For instance: "A wall-eyed jay cracks a cherry's / skull against the cheekbone of dusk," and "Cornflower satin, heels on parquetry—she orders / nests for her hair to keep skylarking near, wears the / clouds on her finger to be swallowed in vapor." There are poems that walk the territory of the actual, from mother-loss, which winters the tips of the speaker's hair, to embodiment: "without my cervix I am no less queen / open me, see there's nothing left to give." Indeed this collection is evidence of a queendom that has been cultivated via solitude, loss, and time. "For years," she writes, "her poemwork involved dipping arrows / into tinctures of monkshood. Beneath her shawl of / suffering, she yearned only for two gifts: to be seen, to be understood." With the unveiling of *Shade of Blue Trees*, those gifts have been delivered. **~Diane Seuss**

❧

In *Shade of Blue Trees*, her astonishing debut collection, Kelly Cressio-Moeller weaves an intricate tapestry of imagery from the ferocity of grief, and the litany of disappearances we all inevitably bear, "knowing every single moment / something or someone is leaving." So much to praise in these resonant poems formed from the fissured bedrock of longing and sorrow: "I wanted / to drink a cup of winter…soft blades of mourning," with wry flashes of humor, "this world is running out of virgins." There is nothing extraneous here, there is passion and wisdom, "You taught me / how not to live: all those years you were not dead but / might as well have been." Each poem a hidden grotto to be revisited, "a quiet haunting" in which we may take refuge. ~**Amber Coverdale Sumrall**

☙

In Kelly Cressio-Moeller's debut collection, she escorts us deep into a melancholy forest, a place both familiar and mystical. Californians will recognize much of the terrain: cypress, pampas grass, black bears, rugged coastlines, and fog. Similarly, these moody poems capture our uneasy contemporary era, while reaching their roots deep into myth. Cressio-Moeller makes our burdens of loss and worry subjects of tenderly examined power ("shoulders that ride so high on worry, / they mistake themselves for wings"). Buoyed by the enduring magic of the natural world, these poems pay somber respect to the extraordinary depth of our quotidian heartaches, and to the exquisite beauty and fragility of ordinary days. ~**Laura Cogan**

Acknowledgments

Grateful acknowledgment is made to the editors and staff of these publications, in which the following poems first appeared, sometimes in different forms or with different titles:

Astropoetica: "Away"
Boxcar Poetry Review: "Panels from a Blue Summer"
burntdistrict: "Departure"
Cider Press Review: "Letter to the Low Tide"
Crab Creek Review: "Panels from a Deepening Winter," "Still Life with Persimmons"
Cultural Weekly: "Dusk at Mt. Diablo"
DNA~Dragonfly Press Ezine: "Visitation"
Escape into Life: "Conscious Sedation"
Gargoyle: "Suburban Aubade with French Horn," "Double Helix," "Something to Remember"
Guesthouse: "Panels from a Courtly Spring"
Iodine Poetry Journal: "Inheritance"
Melusine, or Women in the 21st Century: "Southern Gothic"
Menacing Hedge: "Portent Big Sur," "Sacrament"
Pirene's Fountain: "Magnolia Soulangeana," "Irony"
Rattle: "Waiting for Charon in the ER"
Redwood Coast Review: "A Night of One's Own"
Salamander: "Portent with Moonset & Blackbirds"
Sand Hill Review: "Woman in Blue Reading a Letter"
Southern Humanities Review: "Offerings"
Spillway: "Threshold"
Switched-on Gutenberg: "Among Other Things"
THRUSH Poetry Journal: "Meditations on Disappearing," "Pelagic," "Ithaka," "Self-Portrait as Empty Reliquary"
Tinderbox Poetry Journal: "On Why I No Longer Sit at the Window Seat on a Train," "Diminuendo"
Valparaiso Poetry Review: "White Stones," "Fig Tree at Big Sur"
Water~Stone Review: "Panels from a Celestial Autumn"
ZYZZYVA: "Begin & End at Big Sur"

Reprints:

"Departure" reprinted for Susan F. Glassmeyer's *April Gifts: Little Pocket Poems*, mailer, under the title "Threshold II"

"Double Helix" reprinted at *Cultural Weekly*, nominated for a Pushcart Prize

"Fig Tree at Big Sur", A Room of Her Own Foundation anthology, *Waves, a Confluence of Women's Voices*, edited by Diane Gilliam, 2020

"Ithaka" reprinted at *As It Ought To Be* blog, nominated for a Pushcart Prize and Best of the Net from *THRUSH Poetry Journal*

"On Why I No Longer Sit at the Window Seat on a Train" reprinted at *As It Ought To Be* blog

"*Magnolia Soulangeana*" reprinted at *Cave Moon Press* blog and *First Water: Best of Pirene's Fountain* anthology

"Meditations on Disappearing" appeared on *Verse Daily*

"Waiting for Charon in the ER" reprinted, translated into Italian by Alessandra Bava at *Patria Letteratura*; reprinted in Tresha Haefner's book *Method and Mystery: A Research-Based Guide to Teaching Poetry, Plus Sixty Deepening Prompts for You and Your Students* published by The Poetry Salon

"White Stones" used in Tresha Haefner's ecourse *How to Think Like a Poet* via The Poetry Salon

With Gratitude:

Heartfelt gratitude goes to my editors, Kelli Russell Agodon and Annette Spaulding-Convy, for their amazing care, support, and for seeing my work as worthy. I'm honored to be part of the Two Sylvias Press family.

I am indebted to the extraordinary Diane Seuss for reaching out through the fog and pulling me to shore. Her generosity of spirit, keenest eyes and ears, and impeccable critique carried this book over the finish line. Among the many things, Di, thank you for teaching me how to wield an axe, believe in my work again, and, above all, for our friendship. From the bottom of my heart xx

To my trusted, brilliant, patient, hand-holding manuscript readers (through many iterations!): Francesca Bell, Amber Coverdale Sumrall, Jessica Goodfellow Ueno, Ami Kaye, Veronica Kornberg, Stephanie McCarthy, Stefan Moeller, Christine Monihan, Diane Seuss, Molly Spencer, and Helen Vitoria—your time, attention, and cogent commentary have meant more than I can possibly say.

Poetry dearhearts, confidants, lifelines—love and deepest gratitude for your friendship, wisdom, inspiration, kindness, and unflagging support: Mimi Ahern, Claire Åkebrand, Sally Ashton, Francesca Bell, the Big Sur Land Mermaids [Alanna Alter, Julia Alter Canvin, Martha Clark Scala, Amber Coverdale Sumrall, Catherine Enos, Kathleen Flowers (of blessed memory), and Robin Somers], the Circlers (Kara Arguello, Joanne Rocky Delaplaine, Veronica Kornberg, Catherine Latta, Nancy L. Meyer, Nancy Mohr, Stephanie Pressman, and Mary Lou Taylor), Susan Elbe (of blessed memory), Keisha Gallegos, Jessica Goodfellow Ueno, Erica Goss, the Graces (Tracy Cressio, Stephanie McCarthy, Patti Mena, and Debbie Olsen), Nancy Hightower, Julie Hughes, Rebecca Janicki, Ami Kaye, Christine Monihan, Luisa Oliveira Sunderland, Connie Post, Erin Redfern, Sally Rosen Kindred, the Salonnières (Siobhán Ellis, Marilyn Fogel, Sybil Hudson, Zita Macy, Ann Myhre, Minoti Pakrasi, and Rosemary Van Lare), Diane Seuss, Sarah J. Sloat, Molly Spencer, Helen Vitoria, and Hilary Wheeler.

To all whom I was lucky enough to share sacred circle space with over the many years in Amber's retreats at the New Camaldoli Hermitage—my wholehearted thanks to the loveliest fellow retreatants, to the monks for silence and nourishing meals, Therese Gagnon for her incredible baked treats, to Big Sur's coastline, the Santa Lucia Mountains, Point Lobos, pine and redwood sisters, cypress brothers, the moon, stars, night sky, and my beloved Pacific for her beauty, power, magic, and peace.

To the Willow Glen Library Third Thursday Open Mic Poets (and the previous Willow Glen Books)—the very first group I read my poems to in public. Thank you for the sincerest welcome and acceptance over the years.

Thanks to Poetry Center San José for continuing to sponsor these events for poets to gather, share, and learn.

To the beautiful Glass Lyre Press family—thank you for your continued good cheer and warmth through the ether. You're all amazing.

To the hosts who asked me to read at events over the years, I can't tell you how much that meant to me. Bea Garth you were the very first to give me a reading and publication. Thank you for such early belief in my work and, therefore, me. And to all who ventured out and braved Bay Area traffic to attend readings and events. Huge thanks! I know how challenging that is.

To the hardworking editors and staff of the publications who gave these poems wonderful homes before resting between these covers—thank you for making time and space for my work. Sincere thanks to poet and editor Alessandra Bava for her Italian translations of my poems and weekly Twitter love on a loop!

To the whip-smart, sweet, supportive friends I'm connected with on social media, I send deepest thanks for motivating messages, thoughtful notes, and for commenting on or sharing my work. None of it went unnoticed or unappreciated.

To Laura Cogan, Amber Coverdale Sumrall, and Diane Seuss for saying yes and adding their generous words to this book. I am unbelievably grateful and lucky.

To Helen Vitoria for her incredible talent in creating my book trailer, so beautiful I continue to play it. Thank you for your work and always sharing in my excitement.

Andreea Braescu—thank you for allowing use of your gorgeous art/image for the cover and your genuine excitement about it.

Big love and sincere thanks to my beloved, crazy, wonderfully supportive family, in the US and abroad—all the Cressios, Hugheses, McCarthys, Moellers, Nortons, and Stokeses: I'm grateful for every one of you.

Stephanie, I promise, this is the very last version. Lee, thanks for teaching me to protect myself with the palm heel strike xx

To Ron and Nina, my late parents, who always knew I had a book in me; I wish you were here to hold this in your hands; I feel your tender strength continue from beyond.

To my darling basset hounds—Stella who was here for every line, and Ruby who celebrated the publication, both the best under-the-desk foot warmers and true comforts.

To the beautiful menfolk I share my life with, the very best of me—Stefan, this book would not exist without your love, humor, and continuous encouragement…not to mention your serious coffee making skills and incredible first reader catches. Hendrik and Anton, thank you for your support and understanding. A thousand thanks would not suffice.

And to you, dear reader, thank you—again and again.

For my parents, Ron and Nina Cressio, of blessed memory.

✶✶

*Für Stefan, auf immer und ewig, "i love you much (most beautiful darling) /
more than anyone on the earth and I / like you better than everything in the sky"
~ E.E. Cummings*

∞

For Hendrik and Anton, all my love.

Table of Contents

Death is woven in with the violets...
~ Virginia Woolf

PORTENT WITH MOONSET & BLACKBIRDS

For a long time I wanted
        to drink a cup of winter,
                to become tipsy on early
                        dark & longer starshine.

The thinning light
        my favorite ether.
                These days I am uncertain, dead
                        reckoning my way through—

surrendering to mystery
        & surprise of mapless navigation.
                That fistful of blackbirds
                        thrown across my wind-

shield? I don't know what
        their flurried wingbeats
                were trying to tell me;
                        not every moment

is a teacher, in the same way patience
        does not mean measured inaction.
                I'm only a woman who con-
                        tinues to bury her dead—

wearing a clenched jaw that expects
        diamond dust from crown crush;
                shoulders that ride so high on worry,
                        they mistake themselves for wings.

I've never liked what I was
         called, even though
                  my father named me
                           & my name in his voice

was the last word I'd hear
         him speak. Last night,
                  I went to bed feeling hope-
                           less & profoundly lonely.

I left the curtains open wide.
         Sleep plowed a ragged field of un-
                  even rows—but in the morning's
                           early darkness, the fullest moon

poured its cool, bewitching light
         into the small bowls of my room & garden.
                  As it hung impossibly low over
                           the Pacific, I drank & drank.

DEPARTURE

Two months ago, I scribbled poem notes on hospital paper towels—

    my mother dying, snowed on morphine, pneumonic lungs sinking

        boats she wanted no one to bail out. Her small hands inflated twice

            their size as if to keep afloat. The echocardiogram detailed

            a scalloped shell of aortic waves, mitral valve murmurations.

        How many secrets did her starlings harbor?

    To mark each changing hour, Pegasus, nailed midflight

on the beige wall, shook his mane from side to side.

I consulted the meadow priests of purple thistle whose prickly

    heads provided no comfort. They said, *Death is a circling*

        wolf. There will be no one left to call you by your full name.

            Grief falls in rain-whipped sheets; the shadows of the dead

        weigh more than you know. I looked to the night sky

    for a comet tail, but only cold stars stared back, unblinking.

  That month my mother died, I did not bleed and the tips of my hair

wintered. A book finished inside me; my ink tongue froze.

PANELS FROM A DEEPENING WINTER

The world is so loud. Keep falling. I'll find you.
~Kate Bush

✦

Veils of clouds replace the mountain's ghost-blue face: snow and fog, a sky of ice—a quiet haunting, a brumal embrace.

✦

The blacksmith's wife speaks to him in peach-leaf embers, her timbre sparks and dissolves. Every hammer swing forges the horn of his anviled heart, hot as the infection that took her. She's stolen the wind's fingers and fists—in his hair, at his door. He sleeps in a leather apron, the window open—their winter plums in a copper bowl.

Harnessing broad-nosed oxen, he blames the tears in his eyes on the rain in his head, fingerprints the breeze carrying her neck and hair: hyssop and coriander. He opens his box of mountains, takes her ivory comb, wraps it in the small dreams of winter wrens then lines his waistcoat with her ashes. Cloven hoofbeats and chimney plumes herald the violet dusk.

At midnight he walks alone into the antlered forest, surrounded by the dampened knock of naked branches, cups a buckeye for luck. In a moonlit clearing he makes a promise to a white moose kneeling in the snow, opens his arms ready to catch the night as it falls.

◆◆

Atop the hill by the watermill, black sheep prune the waist-high heather. A jackdaw flock wheels overhead collecting cufflinks of memory for her cabinet of treasures.

◆◆

The year stops for no one. Since he has gone, everything is hourglass: thin-throated and bottomless. The sun, a Siberian king—the moon undressed, in flames. She misses how he shifted the air around her, bent the light into haloed hexagons: honeycomb, snowflake, tortoise shell— the geometry of love.

In the lonely light of morning, shy crocus and taciturn birds surrender to snow. Flashes of him behind her—back to chest, his arms on either side— their hands in a basin of water, thumbs pressed into the lungs of pomegranate halves, releasing a thousand tiny hearts.

Who are you? *I am the feather on the path, blue shadows dragging the hills, a steadfast current clearing your riverbed.* And why have you come? *Because you have asked me to.*

◆◆◆

With red-petaled cries, open mouths of cyclamen confess in winter. Her scarlet sails fall fast asleep in delicate cages—the broken mast, the dream now splintered.

◆◆◆

The night before her journey, she kneels at the frozen Lake of Forgotten Bells, disguises sorrow as a sparrow's heart, offers her silk tongue to the oyster moon. As a child, she lost her compass in the village field and has never found a way.

The wind wears heels tonight. The stars are not made of clouds and dust but bright bones and flowers. She knows the oars of her long boat will never reach the shore.

Back home in the walled garden, it is quiet in the way that only winter is. Euphoric movement— the wings of an immaculate crane, ascending higher and higher, and then all is white.

WHITE STONES

Quiet as night

Twisting in the breeze of stars,

You place feathers for me to find:

In the garden, my book bag, a desk drawer.

These soft blades of mourning

Carve a space in the air for us to meet.

Sweet silence. Sweet stillness.

Tonight, on this cliffside path,

My flashlit footsteps make

The small stones speak.

I cannot see it but the ocean is here

Like the heaviness your absence leaves,

An anchor sinking, unraveling its chain.

There is beauty in this—a merciful peace

That disrobes the shadows around me,

Steadies my gait.

As I wander among the cypress in the dark,

You are stones painted white, marking my way

Home to a place I've never lived,

Under constellations I've never known.

AWAY

Overnight earth's hourglass

turns round spilling

ocean into sky, starshine

against seafloor black—

a radiant play of brilliants.

Just there a swarm of blue stars,

their nebulous cluster fixed over us.

Such quiet wonder only possible

because of the darkness.

We have been away from each other

for the sigh of a day.

Instinctively, my palm searches

for the length of your spine, fingertips

count vertebrae and breaths.

In this canyon of distance,

the ripening desire for home

hangs low enough to bite.

Instead I stare and stare,

neck bends back surrendering my throat

to cosmic strands of pearls,

knowing every single moment

something or someone is leaving,

redshifting in elongated waves.

There is no siren's wail

coming closer in alarm

then fading to an unhearable hum.

By the time the horizon dims, it is too late.

THRESHOLD

Bottle me honey and sea salt for the journey.

    Somewhere there must be green grass and palominos

        grazing. A cabin with light in the window or the warm

            scent of cedar. I am lost in a thicket of stone trees;

                ancestral ghosts inhabit the bark — their tongues reluctant bells.

        My hands run over fossil and limestone

    trailing distilled language, sacred music.

I will make candles from tallow and ash,

set fire to whatever will burn.

    Sometimes all that remains is rebirth.

    Play me a mournful tune, O Wind Harp,

        in this fallow field at dusk.

            My ears are deaf to wild birdsong.

            When it returns, I will have something to say.

        Soon, night shall shed its woven husk —

    bringing brighter brightness.

And still I stumble inwards toward the dark,

    a disquiet doe threadbare between the sun standing still

        and the world asking it to leave. I await my turn at the word well.

            With each sheet of parchment, the skin at my wrists

                begins to thin. Big Sur stars harbor in my veins.

        The days hold their breath

    summoning an ancient silence, an intimacy —

the way the moon makes love to the ocean

or the mountain mirrors the slope

    of my father's shoulder

        as it disappears into the sea.

MEDITATIONS ON
DISAPPEARING

i

don't waste

    the sun's time

start growing   a beard

for winter   summer's

skinned-plum knees ripen

    just below the eyelet hem

between the laundry & the bourbon

study corsetry & lacewings

speak of floating ribs   pinioned wings

discover where birds go to die

a series of open-mouthed pours

separating daylight :: & :: prey

gone is gone is gone

ii

once   thieves tiptoed by candlelight

left impressions in wax   blue

sweat from copper poisoning

blackened cork   a bead of oil

tried to fill the furrows & whorls

with another's life

fingerprints lay bare   but won't tell

where the bodies are buried

iii

I met a woman who was mauled

by a black bear   arms lost

hands replaced by hooks

at parties she says her name   relives

the story as if by script   forty

years on   the bear is still alive

CONSCIOUS SEDATION

Slipping under, I remember me—
a girl neglectful of the sky,

wearing red Mary Janes
and a full set of teeth. Now I walk

through shadows of tall trees, their clinquant
boughs gold and silver crowned.

My breath warm on the pane of a glasswing
butterfly as I lean in to hear the heartbeat

of a wych elm, frisk the bark for a pig's tooth
to replace the tender rogue in my jaw—

another gone before it is taken,
another taken before I am gone.

VISITATION

I walked along a paved road
high above the Pacific, and two

nimble deer appeared beside me on the hill.
I stopped to look at them.

They stopped to look at me.
And when they moved, their hooves

tapped a familiar code
only I could decipher.

I understood those deer
were my parents,

checking in to say, *Your life
is not invisible to us.*

*And the love we always had
for you, continues—*

*Even now, as we nibble on low hanging branches.
Even now, as we climb higher up the hill.*

*Even now, as we turn our heads away—
leaving, again.*

{ II }

BEGIN & END AT BIG SUR

See the coral dust over the mountains? The hooves of sunrise horses
are in full gallop.

No one told the bees it was a silent retreat.

Look at my palm—where these slivers of heart & fate intersect:
you are here.

What if a woodpecker has a migraine?

A dying ash—its upturned, barren candelabras still majestic.

My trailer's sliding door is stuck, gives a little more each morning.

First whale pod sighting, cerulean breach & swirl—worth the sunstroke.

I'm convinced this sow bug crossing my path is the same one who made
love to my eraser last year.

A schoolgirl crush on ponderosa pines: spiky hair, limber branches,
muscled cones like silent birds.

In late afternoon, pampas grass tapers shine silver as the hair in my brush.

Starburst spores float over my shoulder—someone's made a wish upon
a dandelion clock. I turn around; no one is there.

I hold the sun's hand until it falls asleep.

The ocean creates its own light.

AMONG OTHER THINGS

A spoon left on the rest from her morning egg.

The calendar was wrong. It was nothing like spring.

A field of headstones asks *Have You Seen Me?*

An aria, Puccini's "Nessun dorma" sung by Lanza, looped repeatedly.

A small black suitcase surfaced in a pond.

Close my eyes and the freeway sounds like the ocean.

Unspeakable things can happen in churches.

The scent of freesias, chloroform.

She came home from school and kissed her mother.

The coffee had gone cold.

Daydreaming in Italian: chiaroscuro, baldacchino, sprezzatura.

The tree's arms hold her in the indigo lap of sky.

She was dead before they knew she was missing.

How ordinary this day was to be.

LETTER TO THE LOW TIDE

I see what you're doing—vanishing   to make me feel less alone.

   Your thin skin easy   in the moon's quiet pocket, scuff

                               of pale blue.

     I, too, want

                 to unhook myself from shore.

We are not narrow-hearted,   simply responding to gravity's dark crest.

   Wait for the rush,

     unseen but quickening, as the high-spired shell surrenders its song

              only when brought close.

INHERITANCE

I

Before he was an altar boy,
he was an altered boy.
His head a globe of sable
curls to remind her of the girl
she wished he'd been.

When the ringlets were shorn,
they dropped like thick ropes
leaving him untethered, floating
toward the planet of a man
he would become.

As he grew taller, branching sinuous arms,
he became her workhorse and whipping boy—
bruised deep by his grandfather's transgressions.
Shelter was found within neighborhood
kitchens and the sacristy of priests.

My father married young, hastily
eloping with my mother in the neighboring county—
his own mother's disapproval stuffed
into his blue suit pocket; my sister tucked
into our mother's teenage womb.

II

Before she was a mother who loved
at arm's length, she was a shattered girl
who grew into a mosaic of glass shards—
all angles and hard jawline framed
by quartz hair and a cutting gaze.

She was born in the high daze
of summer, Wednesday's child
of woe—kept in line by a cat o'
nine tails and her bootlegger
father's constant inattention.

He loved miserly, doling out
fragments of his heart
in measured spoons of sugar,
sprinkling a white trail of insanity
for his teen bride and children to follow.

My grandmother married young, secretly
escaping with an older man who looked only at her
eyes instead of her walnut-stained hands.
Her floral dress was borrowed; her intentions were all her own.
In the end, she would wear black longer than white.

III

At her Easter graveside, the earth's open mouth was silent;

my father's lips cut a thin line on his face. The only sound

the slow reel of the casket, unspooling.

IRONY

When your mother dies

the first person

you want to call

is her.

DOUBLE HELIX

I am growing thick in the middle again,

      an avalanche over the waistband.

Those pounds I strong-willed away,

      unwelcomed back into newly upholstered

cells. A scale is unnecessary. Last summer's

      clothes now grab my breasts and thighs

with graceless but determined ardor.

      My corduroys brush and spark.

Strict exceptions become the reckless rules.

      The last pastry or bread slice becomes a second

or third. What am I trying to feed?

      How I green-eye marvel at those women

who sit straight-backed and cross-legged in simple

      chairs, effortless as their unlabored breathing.

My lumbering limbs wince and blush.

      Such slender tenderness my body

has never known. Where to rest when your nest

      of skin feels cold as wintergreen dusk? I think

of my parents riding under the weight

      of themselves, careening down

demented diabetic roads, bread-crumbed days

      spent wiped and bathed as their bodies surrender

to decades of excessive hunting and gathering.

      My sleep plays hopscotch, each night falling

further from the last. I've lost count of the recurring

      dream where a black bear, rearing full height

upon its hind legs, swings inadequate claws

      at a half-hearted moon. All through these nights

of humorless stars, I hear bits of life cry out, each skating

      their separate darkness: a heron's snapped wing,

a loon's lonely wail, my burdened bones.

PORTENT BIG SUR

a vulture flies over the car

through cypress, the Pacific glares

did I run over the baby quail?

pink sweet peas tongue dry grass

stuck in my gums, pin bones from lunch

tears during meditation

limping doe does not return

earring lost

ants in the bed

scorpion's tail striking starry-milk

middle of the night Coast Guard dives

great gray owl warns the spilling moon

migraine fog at 5 a.m.

Monday's twin-yolked egg

                              the vulture circles back

LETTER TO THE RAIN

Come at me with guillotine sheets,
     I will be happy in separation.
Forgive my sadness.
     It's not your fault—your window
taps tender me, the slow dance in fog.
     You bring greening mountains,
phantoms as morning steam
     off fence rails, still I gutter—
candlelight starved for air.

     Remember the pelican who flew
into the schoolyard's field?
     How are you so far from home?
—all of us dreaming coastline
     and cliffside, the phosphorous
veil. *Where to find a safe place*
     in winterbare branches? I think
of him often. How you said nothing
     except in downpour.

I'm not strong, dear Deluge,
     dear Cloudburst, dear Torrent.
During the night you've taken
     the spider's elegant home and made

the lilies shy. You have

      taught me light will not wait,

and yet I cannot be the only one

      who blows the ocean kisses when leaving.

What I know today is if you ask

      me why there are tears in my eyes,

I will tell you it's just the wind.

PANELS FROM A COURTLY SPRING

The leaves around her breathe citrus / and dusk.

I think of you when the last light / glints off

the roof tiles. ~Malinda Markham

✦

You shall be Queen—an Austrian pawn in Versailles. Let's not speak of consuming love, my obedient swan, soon will be time for judgment & lies.

✦

Cornflower satin, heels on parquetry—she orders nests for her hair to keep skylarking near, wears the clouds on her finger to be swallowed in vapor. His passion grows for libraries & locks, intricacies of cogs & clocks beguile him but no cock crows among their orange groves. Pile on the gilt, guilt, geld but no pollen from his anther. Seven years of chaste moons & the sheets are still dry. She would ask him to hold her but doesn't know where his hands have been.

Betwixt the banquets & balls, she's cursed for mounting like a man in buckskin breeches—gossip glitters, then kaleidoscopes, in every mirror. Too many harlequin stairs & wide-open vistas, yet she cannot awaken her homesick lungs. She compares her life to waves, in opulence & roil, but will never see the sea.

Send a letter to my mother—tell her I am trying.

✦✦

O grapes & fermentation, bless your rivers filled with blood, dove & blush. In book of hours & incantations, time unfolds between piping calls of thrush.

✦✦

Fireflies over the meadow, soft spangle of tapers, the hem of her chemise catching on reeds—she carries a small basket of radishes, rubies for shire horses who soft-lip her palm. Here she runs rose-wild, banishes hard eyes & whalebone stays; her mother's voice locked in a lacquer box.

Hope-winged & bud-opened, he waits with flasks of wine & stolen figs; his long coat blankets the ground. They speak of amulets & falcons, parlor games & nightingales—turn yearning's blue fire into a dreamscape fugue. Notes of jasmine & neroli, far-off troubadours garland the air. Leaning into her, his tongue traces small flowers along her throat.

Send a whisper through the lindens to dispel this
tryst.

✦✦✦

No chance remains for this foreigner at court—where rumor reigns the most scapegoating sport. Her confidants & guards draw close at the palace—spry-teeming seachange: empty-bellied, mouthfuls of malice.

✦✦✦

The night of rain is unexpected, flint-eyed & greening—candlelight silhouettes run on high-ceilinged fear. The wilding roars from chamber to chamber, clamber up pastel walls. She's barefoot, racing, barely outrunning the metal clamor of blades & pikes. Hecatomb harvest: errant gardeners chopping down hedgerows, the golden orchard bright with blood.

Send compassion to my daughter, she'll lose her
brother next.

****

O Mother, cool Empress, is this what you imagined for your landlocked girl? No peace in the fortress, no rue-weighted bones? I did what was asked, loyal until I left the world.

****

On the final morning her brave face blooms backwards, under the glade where roots embrace silence, forever-hide her display. She woolgathers in her garden, steady steps; the ordered beds are still but strangely broken with lowering furrows of fresh-turned soil. Bound behind her back, the last hand she held was her own—pale hair shorn close as a lamb's coat, her crown of lost light.

Send a wagon to the square & bring my body home.

{ III }

WOMAN IN BLUE READING A LETTER
after Johannes Vermeer, oil on canvas, c.1663

It was so clear to me that it was almost invisible. ~Neko Case

*

It was mid-afternoon when I arrived in Amsterdam. The flight from California fueled a headache I couldn't shake. I checked into my hotel room, hoping a hot shower would restore me. I was slipping on my robe when I noticed the blinking red light on the room's phone: a message from my mother to call home. Her voice was low, a strange mixture of indecision and sadness. She spoke slowly as though lowering an anchor; there had been an accident. Tommy, close as a brother, was dead: a drunk driver crossed the divider, hit him head-on, the engine in his lap. I don't remember telling her goodbye, hanging up the phone, or getting dressed, but I rode the elevator down and walked the stone-paved streets, shellshocked under a turquoise sky.

**

At the Rijksmuseum, whose rib-vaulted portico reminded me of a Gothic crypt, bicycles sped through the passageway before I entered. Upstairs, Vermeer had a room of his own. I stepped off the hardwood floor and sank deep into blue carpet. She was on the damask wall next to *The Milkmaid*, illuminated by skylight glow—so small, she could fit in my suitcase. But I didn't care about the light or the colors. I didn't care about the woman or the news in her letter. It was the map hanging behind her. The one detail that had seemed incidental before was all I could focus on now—all those meandering lines leading to and away from home.

ITHAKA

Dear Penelope, do you now sleep among the catacombs?

Scarves of white drift over the Aegean—an altar of bottomless blue.

I have gone to the edge of the world and still cannot find you.

Even the olive trees raise their spangled limbs skyward in longing.

Mother Earth slides her abacus beads, conjures storms quick as curses.

When lightning struck, did the boat protect or beckon the bolt?

Island flowers shut their eyes only when the stars disrobe—hope and sorrow held within the same root.

She imagines him bright-toothed and swarthy, but her husband is just sunburned and homesick.

So many suitors holding her skeins—she's woven a trail for her waylaid mariner, long as his beard and her undoing.

In twenty years, she has never asked, *What shall I wish for myself?*

Odysseus wonders, *Do I have the right to return?*

Maids cast offerings to the sea: red rose petals and grape leaves— love and wine all that remain.

SOUTHERN GOTHIC

Sweet mother of pearl and all things holy

but that man jellied her bones — left her higher than

the tall grass of their coupling. Satyr. Bourboned

hoof prints tattooed across summer skin.

How was she to know? 3 X's on his bare-chested

bullseye: buried treasure, barmaid kisses, crosshairs.

No matter which, they left their mark.

A bullet for each of them. Powder burns formed

cul-de-sacs of a triangle. Scalene. No sides equal.

Ventricles gave way like levees his father engineered.

Poets and suicide. It's been done before.

THAT death was mine! Go on then. Git gone.

Sometimes a woman needs to take to her bed.

Burying a lover shook loose her stars. Some yonder-eyed

gaze no longer her own. The offset jaw. A cindered lament.

She continued down lost roads. Planted a curved

wall of bamboo, grew a headful of words. Sylvan light

filtered June — remains.

PANELS FROM A BLUE SUMMER

Listen, I didn't want your tears
in my eyes. ~Alice Fulton

✦

I lack the luster that my lilacs
can muster at any time of year.

✦

A summer of torched moods, bruised
gin—dark as the sea of our newborn,
white waves of woolgathering
mavens in owl-faced conversations.
My mouth blooms bowls of amaranth
and thistle in the melancholy shade of
blue trees.

Outside my window, knots in the
fence stare drunk as bull's eyes.
Concentric ripples landlocked in
dendrochronology like Van Eyck's
triptychs—layers upon layers
of brittle meditations, a peeling
in reverse.

✦✦

Peacocks ring the rotund rotunda,
shadow steps through the steppe from
Dachau to dachas. Up to their knees
in windbreaker trees,
chryselephantined.

♦♦

A wall-eyed jay cracks a cherry's
skull against the cheekbone of dusk.
This world is running out of virgins.
Too many shoes from overstayed
welcomes left by the door. Car-wash
girls with yellow semaphores pistol-
whip July, swallow sunlight
clockwise. Their closed eyes shine
with the kiss of gold coins. In German
the word for poison is Gift.

♦♦♦

To be the leaver or the left, the cleaver
of the cleft—his language a glacier
calving, nouns vanish under ice—the
bereaver, the bereft.

♦♦♦

The spots on his hands form island
chains he visits when lonesome. The
natives there are kind, blowing
memory darts in flashback. An index
finger itches for his revolver's cool
scythe. He tells his story to a nearby
stone, carves one word upon it:

s   o   o   n

◆◆◆◆

She will miss the hiss of every sunset.
All figures in her mirror dissolving as
they near.

◆◆◆◆

The rarest of Norf London birds dies
a hundred times, falling from the
ledge of her skeleton key. Carpet
burns and whiskey dick, the slide of
houndstooth over taffeta. I stretch
along the black watch where secrets
of her beehive find me in notes of
shimmering mica. She tucks her
wings   and   dives.

PELAGIC

A water / unlike any other water ~Joanna Klink

At Point Lobos, a woman mentions she nearly drowned
at Monastery Beach—some days she can still taste brine.

Pleurisy of tissue and wave: kick harder, kick harder.
Grow a third lung, line it with desire. Holdfast. Hold. Fast.

Cormorant deep-dives, belly full of pebbles. Flash your blue
throat to me! Build us a nest, carino, con posidonie e fiori.

Tie the boat in the shallows, hike through dune asters,
a clutch of bees, thick bullwhips beached on black stones.

18th century vaqueros broke mustangs along coastal bluffs, mistook
barking sea lions for wolves. Gray whale cries ghost the cove.

Sway-balanced on driftwood, a great blue heron syncs with my
shipwrecked vertigo, slow motion wingbeats carry her away.

Poseidon chases down the sun. Storm-footed chariot. White-
starred Hippocampi. Coffin bones hammer the seafloor gold.

In the Whaler's Cabin, a man spoke about the sea—
how it took his boy and didn't give him back.

Giant kelp coppers teal water, long garlands wreathe into laurel
crowns as if all Olympus is surfacing.

SACRAMENT

I see the horizon's crimson vein and recall the
stained washcloth in your small room. I thought
(truly this is what I thought) that someone must
have wiped the juice from a freshly cut
watermelon then placed the neatly folded cloth
in the sink. No matter that it was not
watermelon season or that you had died that
morning, dead before your head hit the table.
In that moment before grief rolled up
its sleeves, your dark-eyed daughter
stood before the stainless basin,
wringing the cloth under the tap.

STILL LIFE WITH PERSIMMONS

Slightly taller than a yardstick,

  I spend summer days in my grandparent's

    garden with a boundless

persimmon tree—

  its limbs too high for me to climb.

    In the yard's back corner, a stone grotto:

home for the Virgin Mary.

  Our heights equal, our favorite color midnight

    blue, her cloak's bright paint fading

in the sun. Before her chipped feet, a cloth napkin

  for teacups and frosted cookies.

    Family friends arrive: a couple

with their teenage son—

  black hair and hawk-faced.

    In the garden I offer him

my empty cup; he wipes his mouth

  with the back of his hand and pulls me

    onto his lap. His finger crosses his lips

—our secret—then slides into my daisy print panties.

Mary peers at us over his shoulder—

head tilted in permanent concern,

her alabaster eyes wide and hollow.

FIG TREE AT BIG SUR

Each day leaning

into morning,

five-fingered leaves

wave in unison,

beckon jays

for branch-play.

The youngest leaves

arch green faces upward,

devour sun off the Pacific.

The golden elders

bow closer to earth—

the perfect shape

for water to run

as rain, as fog

down to the root line.

When afternoon rays

light them just right,

they become a ring

of open palms

giving the last

of what they have.

{ IV }

ON WHY I NO LONGER SIT AT THE WINDOW SEAT
ON A TRAIN

It's a good day for a lie-down, overcast
and wet-wooled. Even the rain wants to be horizontal.
I am daydreaming of goose down when I
enter the train, scoot into an open seat,
press my cheek against the streaked window.
The station's soothing voice announces,
Zurückbleiben bitte, someone runs in just before
the doors close, slams me against the side
of the compartment, takes a lungful of my air.
He asks my name, if I *want some fun* back
at his room. I buy time before the next stop,
tell him I'm *Whitney from America*
(anything but my real name in his mouth).
Now he locks his arm through mine and thick
fingers jab my ribs. His leg, an anchor—
his pocked face smirks like he's already
notched his belt.

I imagine the defense move my brother
taught me where I smash my palm heel into
some asshole's nose, shifting bone into brain.
(Where is my Siegfried in this country of the
"Nibelungenlied". What would Kriemhild do?)
My eyes ransack the forest of businessmen,
cutpurses, Hausfrauen, the heroin chic: rows
of enameled faces, cow-dumb, indifferent as teeth.
Let the Ausländer fight it out!
Thigh-grab, elbow-jab, hand-slap—his broken
English splinters the air. Whitney Houston
in my head singing "I Will Always Love You"

on some godforsaken loop as I mentally run through
my list of German imperatives: Hilfe! Polizei!
Vergewaltigung! (a word that takes longer to say
than the act it defines). I backhand him across
the mouth, escape before the doors slam.
He's waving (waving!) through the glass,
a blurry fat-lipped sneer retreating—the air
staccatoed with rasps of my breath. It begins
to hail marbles. Even the gods are throwing stones.

Only later with candlelight und Butterkuchen,
do I resurface to Vivaldi's strings on the radio.
I mention my morning combat-commute.
My host shrugs his shoulders before loading
the Meissen with another helping of Schadenfreude.
He says, *Da muβ man durch*: "one must go through it"—
as if it were a tunnel, something to be run through.

MAGNOLIA SOULANGEANA

i

mistrustful of evergreens.
defined as deciduous was part of the appeal.
every living thing should shed its skin once a year.
one left in the back, nearly dead—perfect, i'll take it.

ii

sculptural as coral, judging by the photo.
slender bare branches promised to proffer dark purple
saucers of tea, goblets of port, depending on my mood.
if she were lipstick, i would name her *violet empress*.

iii

she didn't look like much. a few jaundiced ovals resembled
leaves. six years until she felt strong enough in smooth pewter
skin. long buds broke open in late winter, unexpectedly white
with pink veins, little scars, along tepals soft as well-worn suede.

OFFERINGS

I buy him just before the surgery: talisman
carved from a single piece of suar wood.
Eyes closed, legs crossed, one hand in his lap,
the other raised to his chest—index fingers and thumbs
forming perfect O's. There is nothing to fear.
His hands tell me so.

I carry him to the kitchen counter,
an infant ready for his sink bath,
squeeze thick lines of salve onto my bare
fingers—a blend of beeswax and mineral oil,
the same mixture I use on my cutting boards.
Each feathered pass of my fingertips reveals
glowing dark-grained skin. I massage
deep folds of his robe,
lobes of his elongated ears,
riverbed curls on his head,
the silver dollar knot in his back.

I rub his chest and recall childhood
bouts of bronchitis; my mother
slathering my chest with ointment
from the neon green Mentholatum jar,
then placing a square of warmed flannel, white with haloes

of small red stars and pinking-sheared edges,

atop the quivering plane of my lungs—

eyelids surrender, camphor-infused fumes

rise up through my nostrils, hit the back

of my throat, curve air into barely-open passageways.

I leave him wrapped overnight in his creamy vernix.

In the morning, I wipe away the excess—

clean as the surgeon's cut.

DUSK AT MT. DIABLO

The drive to Devil Mountain takes only half an hour.

He was a beautiful boy. Everyone agreed—including his killer.

Visitors should plan to be in their vehicles before sunset.

All her life she was quick to flame and smolder.

Note typed. Animals euthanized. Biding her time.

They hiked a short trail to Lookout Point. She snapped his photo.

The darkest hours can pass in daylight.

She hated her ex-husband more than she loved her son.

A starless sky still shines as bright.

Three bullets when one would have been enough.

Years pass. We shelve our rage.

Throats of crows caw and scatter.

The beat of wings carries over the valley.

DIMINUENDO

My

parents'

music

grows

softer

and

softer

until

I

must

kneel,

place

my

ear

to

the

ground.

SUBURBAN AUBADE WITH FRENCH HORN

The demons don't like fresh air. What they like best is if you stay
in bed with cold feet. ~Ingmar Bergman

This morning more leafblower than birdsong. Autumn chills
stained glass leaves, fissures orange where summer used to live.
My body carries me over cement trails, breaks through tethers
of glistening web, first down the street. The neighbor's yard

punctuated with foil, gauze, playing cards—curiosities stuck in dry
knee-high weeds. An arm of Bermuda grass, suburban kelp, catches
my laces, tries to pull me down into its resentful sea. As a teen, her
parents made her mow the blighted patch where lawn used to be.

A few houses down, the garage door of the quiet blue house is open.
The wife sculpts her juniper tams as though they are giant bonsai,
each cut precise, unerring—a week of mornings to shape the hedges
into great waves. She disappears before 9 a.m. I don't know her name.

I round the corner toward the elementary school my children
have outgrown. Car lines narrow the street; all the parents bow
to phones. One child's science project has lost its cell membrane
in the boxwood. There isn't enough time to create a second skin.

Side-stepping puddles of goldenrain lanterns, I hear Brahms' "Horn Trio"
playing from an open window. Notes ricochet off the freeway's barrier
wall, trapeze through the air. When I was small, my mother taught
me about the French horn. Her dawns now an hourglass of yesterdays.

Despite the drought, some lawns mushroom with death caps, enough
to poison the entire block: *Goodbye, sex offenders! So long, neighbors*
who leave their howling dog outside all night! Farewell, fans of insomniac
home improvement! Sweat darkens my underwire.

Back home, from my kitchen window the hills look blue
in the arms of an old moon. I baptize eggs for breakfast—
already morning detaches,

> floats toward night's throat.

A NIGHT OF ONE'S OWN

Make a wish and a dandelion explodes.

There is no precedent for this.

I smoked my annual cigarette in January. Virginia rolled her own.

Some words can only be written at night.

Two boys tucked in a redwood cathedral. Slow breaths on the cliff of sleep.

Paper sucks ink like blood into sand. The process.

Dark chocolate. Pinot noir. More please.

I could drink a case of Joni.

Candlelight viewed through a steamy shower door. Midnight lantern.

A clutch of barn owls clamors for food. My basset hound sleeps.

I take odd comfort reading even pages.

Virginia wrote only in purple ink that even the Ouse could not fade.

I ache for sex, as night moves over bodies entwined.

This is what I tell myself whistling in the dark, singing to the moon.

Why would I ever erase this?

WAITING FOR CHARON IN THE ER

Bad news is always arriving. ~Adrienne Rich

Make a fist.

The ambulance ride

begins with a deep poke

into a surprised vein.

Open. Close.

Time-lapse photography.

A lotus unfurling

in my palm. I see

sunlight breaking through crowns

of eucalyptus, breathe

oxygen through a tube.

I'd recognize his face

anywhere: paramedic Gauguin,

Civilization is what makes you sick.

Is that why your Christs are yellow and green?

Yes, and blue trees.

What of the red door in the forest?

We are never out of the woods.

Gurneys glide gondola-quiet

through corridored canals.

An oarsman ferries me

into an X-ray room.

His shark tooth bracelet clangs

against the metal buoy.

I want to dive

into his seafoam scrubs,

breaststroke into March.

The doctor orders a rainbow

belt of slender vials.

She pockets my blood

in her jungle print top, swings

on a vine, disappears

into Rousseau's foliage. I don't

see her again for 2 hours.

She's consulted the gorilla

who was sitting on my chest.

I eat red Jell-O with a spork.

Time drifts through saline solution.

A slow drip counts the day's small hours.

I have the room to myself.

So tempting just to lie

there waiting, stock-still

with a coin in my mouth.

SELF-PORTRAIT AS EMPTY RELIQUARY

no saint has ever lived here

                the ultrsound: myomas dine by an open fire

body-truthing the bog: dead leaves & asphodel, the strangest fruit,
the never-born

             thumb-worn rosary—beads now stick in my teeth

is barren ground any less sacred?

      silver-leaf my insides, place a candle in my hollow, follow, fallow

          even broken glass refracts light

                    suture—specter—sepulcher

but look what you have *made* in fall's gold air—hectares plowed,
harrowed, hallowed

                stone webs of scar-tissue tracery

without my cervix I am no less queen

            open me, see there's nothing left to give

to no longer smell of blood

                no saint will ever live here

PANELS FROM A CELESTIAL AUTUMN

i will wade out / till my thighs are steeped in burn-
ing flowers / i will take the sun in my mouth / and leap
into the ripe air
~E.E. Cummings

✦

One piecemeal boy made whole in the woods—
moonflower solace, embered-air haven—a soothing
quiet, unlike home, welcomed even by an unkindness
of ravens.

✦

Before his first shave, he fell from oaken arms. The
storm snapped the sky's back, took the shape of a
throat shouting flames. Between flash & clap,
anxiety's flutterings burnished his gut taut. Jupiter
held the current easy in his hand, slipped it through
the lad from collar to hip. The ground forced smoke
from his wounds, slowed air & sound. Small clouds
of mournful duskywings haloed over his brokenness:
You will mend, they promised, *You will mend.*

Over the years, the bolt captured by his body cleaved another tree into his chest—a raised asterism rivered across ribs & shoulder; its bare branches needling as he grew. Later, lovers trace the tattooed lace of blue-black wrens; scar-feathers rise & fall with every breath.

As both Daphne & Apollo, the arborist chases himself deeper through thick sorrel, wild-astered loam—buries galaxies of quartz for bright vines to root. By vespers, the crows' beauty-doomed calls remind him he's sewn together only with acorns & lightning.

body as dying star, shattered bone temple, an uppercut, as dieback, a tuning fork—body as blade singing through wheat

✦✦

You sparrowed off to another land, another language—presuming I was simply an instrument to unstring. Listen now, neighbor-boy, a girl can harvest memory & I remember everything.

✦✦

I was born when the spark was fading, a gibbous face turned her cold gaze elsewhere. Saturn called me from its hexagon storm, violent winds churning for years; we had an understanding. Above rooftops, over houses, sheds & huts, cycles of abuse exposed in isolated edifices, betrayal atop a hunter green chesterfield. The universe laden with sleepless planets, their flocks of rings tended & ordered. Yet no witness that gray day—where was my shepherd moon? Where was his?

The flashes arrive with autumn loneliness: corduroy chafe, fingers raking thigh, brazen grazing— repressed recollections collage into interior fractures, tidal locking of body & memory cuff together in tethered spin, peeling bark, a hawthorn howling. In Greek, the word for "eclipse" means to abandon, to darken, to cease to exist. I tell my girl-self each time she lights a candle in this dark, *You've made a small fire.*

body as mosaic of dead leaves, cindered coronet, an abscess, a malgrown antler, body as torn pocket that once carried joy

✦✦✦

For years, her poemwork involved dipping arrows into tinctures of monkshood. Beneath her shawl of suffering, she yearned only for two gifts: to be seen, to be understood.

✦✦✦

Lake-eyed & wolf-bit, she dead reckons the hardscape of illness & rough sleep, learns to distrust October's hue. Solar flares persimmon cheek & neck—Venusian heat floods her limbs, transforms joints into gourds. She slides the windows wide— her tear-toned calls telescope across the Sea of Longing. She holds her breath for an answer like nightfall awaits the stars.

Somehow, she is always preparing for winter— pleading for unseasonal snow or strong gusts to cover tracks, dressing in layers to prevent cleaving. Wind-torn, ash-weak: scatter, scatter, scatter—perhaps he views broken things more beautiful. All her hollows planed by years of neglect. And her bones—even those. I dream of her happiness: opening a fresh notebook under an almond arbor, legs crossed in a yellow cane chair, a quiet cup of tea as a lone blue orchard bee ravishes the last bloom.

body as forgotten island, nation of white flags, an
ocean of driftwood & stone, a windharp—cliffside,
body as plate glass under troubled horses

✦✦✦✦

Stardom & gold bluster round musicians' crowns & cozy sycophants who wheedle. Always at their beck & call for any strain of benumbing—be it pill, pipe, glass, or needle.

✦✦✦✦

She sings Christmas carols in September to speed the year along, foggy in the black hole of addiction's damp sleeves—organza skin, grisaille visage. No longer did she want to live through this. U-Haul packed & ready for home. She left her radiant basslines as lodestars for others to follow.

Moonrise to moonset is a day of waiting for the light to disappear. That last push of heaven-dust honeyed her veins—euphoric in the bathtub's cupped palm. How close she was to clean, a getaway, the tender scent of hay. Like all satellites hurtling in this graveyard orbit, she will never land.

body as pincushion cape, Mercury in retrograde, an
amber bottle on the sill, a regal supernova, body as
skirt of hair falling from a loosened knot

◆◆◆◆◆

In dreams, we roam the moors—wandering a veil's length apart. A galleon's spade-shaped anchors tombstone the heather, pattern a strange field of upside-down hearts.

◆◆◆◆◆

O Mother, how I understand you better through my own ripening. Lately, my body's not fit for comfort or migration, only worried unraveling. A chime in hard rain twists to & fro from *tried* to *tired*. I cursed your curtailing, spun a labyrinth from unspoken apologies—is that why my head feels nebula, a burgundy helix of helium & dust? You taught me how not to live: all those years you were not dead but might as well have been.

Bats & hawk moths visit night flowers when you
return; I'd know your rustle of complex comfort
anywhere. *Grieving is also a form of dying*, you say,
Turn up the collar of mourning a day too many &
at duskfall the coachman will arrive at your door—
the latch turns, stairs unfold; your mouth full
of polished jet.

body as first leaf turning, bonfire of regret, an
undiscovered constellation, a volley of opal-tailed
comets, body as a place of shining

SOMETHING TO REMEMBER

Darkness does not hunger for anything.
It has everything it needs. The ribs
of shadows are fat with secrets
of the living and the dead. It never
wallows in loneliness. Never says
leave a message for me if you can.
It doesn't care about your tongue
of honey and stars; your breath
of apples and wine. It's busy
quilting corners of indifference
and will return again and again.
As you go from room to room
cloaking your mirrors for winter,
let the coldness you feel at the nape
move in like fog, shawling you
in her gown of gray beads—listen
when she whispers: *If you are patient,*
your eyes will adjust to the dark.

Notes

The dedication line to Stefan is from poem 45 of the *95 Poems* section ['i love you much (most beautiful darling)'] of *E.E. Cummings: The Complete Poems 1904-1962*. New York, NY: Liveright Publishing Corporation, 1991.

This collection's epigraph is from Virginia Woolf's book *The Waves*. New York, NY: Harcourt, Inc., 1931.

I.

"Portent with Moonset & Blackbirds": The phrase *For a long time I wanted* is from W.S. Merwin's poem "After School" from his collection, *The Rain in the Trees*. New York, NY: Knopf, 1988.

"Panels from a Deepening Winter": The epigraph comes from the song "Snowflake" written by Kate Bush from her album *50 Words for Snow*. Fish People/EMI Records, 2011. Part 3 of the poem is for Malinda Markham.

"White Stones" is for my father.

"Away": The term *play of brilliants* is from architectural lighting designer Richard Kelly.

II.

"Among Other Things" is in memory of Sandra Renee Cantu (2001-2009).

"Panels from a Courtly Spring": The epigraph is from Malinda Markham's poem "First Received" from her collection *Ninety-Five Nights of Listening*. New York, NY: Mariner Books/Houghton Mifflin Company, 2002.

III.

"Woman in Blue Reading a Letter": The epigraph comes from the song "Middle Cyclone" written by Neko Case from her album of the same name. ANTI-, 2009.

"Ithaka": The line *What shall I wish for myself?* is a reworking of Mary Oliver's line *and what shall I wish for, for myself,* from her poem "In Praise of Craziness, of a Certain Kind" from her *New and Selected Poems: Volume Two.* Boston, MA: Beacon Press, 2005.

"Southern Gothic": *THAT death was mine!* is a quote from Anne Sexton from Diane Middlebrook's book *Anne Sexton: A Biography.* Boston, MA: Houghton Mifflin Company, 1991. The poem is for C.D. Wright and Frank Stanford.

"Panels from a Blue Summer": The epigraph is from Alice Fulton's poem "Fair Use" from her collection *Felt.* New York, NY: W.W. Norton & Co., 2001. The line *dies a hundred times* is a variation of Amy Winehouse's line *I died a hundred times* from her song "Back to Black" from her album of the same name. Island Records, 2006. Part 3 of the poem is for my father; Part 4 is for Amy Winehouse.

"Pelagic": The epigraph is taken from Joanna Klink's poem "The Eventides" from her collection *Circadian.* New York, NY: Penguin Books, 2007. The Italian line *con posidonie e fiori* translates to "with seagrass and flowers" with thanks to Alessandra Bava.

IV.

"Dusk at Mt. Diablo" is in memory of Adam Findley Williams (1993-2009).

"Suburban Aubade with French Horn": The epigraph is a quote from Ingmar Bergman from the documentary film *Bergman Island* by Marie Nyreröd, 2004.

"A Night of One's Own": The line *I could drink a case of Joni* is a variation of Joni Mitchell's line *I could drink a case of you* from her song "A Case of You" from her album *Blue*. Reprise Records, 1971.

"Waiting for Charon in the ER": The epigraph is from Adrienne Rich's poem "In the Woods" from *The Fact of a Doorframe: Poems 1950-2001*. New York, NY: W.W. Norton & Co., 2002. *Civilization is what makes you sick* is a quote widely attributed to Paul Gauguin and is a pervasive theme in his writings; however, a direct quote of this in French is difficult to find. It is most likely derived from part of a letter Gauguin wrote to August Strindberg while still in Paris on February 5, 1895: "Civilisation dont vous souffrez" ("Civilization from which you suffer"). The letter is quoted from *The Writings of a Savage: An Anthology of Writing by Gauguin*, edited by Daniel Guérin, translation by Eleanor Levieux. New York, NY: Paragon House Publishers, 1990.

"Panels from a Celestial Autumn": The epigraph is from E. E. Cummings' poem "Crepescule" from *Eight Harvard Poets*. New York, NY: Laurence J. Gomme, 1917. The etymology of 'eclipse' is from Wikipedia contributors. "Eclipse." *Wikipedia, The Free Encyclopedia*. Wikipedia, The Free Encyclopedia, 25 Aug. 2017. The word *beauty-doomed* is indebted to Jane Siberry's song "Morag" from her album *Angels Bend Closer*. CD Baby, 2016. Part 3 of the poem is for Molly Spencer; Part 4 is for Kristen Pfaff.

"Something to Remember": The line *leave a message for me if you can* is from Chase Twichell's poem "To the Reader: Polaroids" from her collection *The Snow Watcher*. San Francisco, CA: Ontario Review Press, 1998. The poem is for Mark Strand.

Kelly Cressio-Moeller was born in San José, California, where she has lived her whole life with exception of 4 years spent in Hamburg, Germany. She holds a BA degree in Humanities from San José State University where she also completed extensive graduate coursework in Art History. She is a poet, visual artist, and loves to play the drums. Her poems have been nominated for Pushcart Prizes, Best New Poets, Best of the Net and have appeared widely in journals and at literary websites including *Crab Orchard Review, Escape into Life, Gargoyle, Guesthouse, North American Review, Poet Lore, Radar Poetry, Salamander, Tinderbox Poetry Review, THRUSH Poetry Journal, Valparaiso Poetry Review, Water~Stone Review,* and *ZYZZYVA,* among others. She participates in numerous poetry readings throughout the Bay Area. Since 2015, she is an associate editor at Glass Lyre Press. She lives in the Bay Area with her husband, two sons, and their basset hound. *Shade of Blue Trees* is her first poetry collection. www.kellycressiomoeller.com

Publications by Two Sylvias Press:

The Daily Poet: Day-By-Day Prompts For Your Writing Practice
by Kelli Russell Agodon and Martha Silano (Print and eBook)

The Daily Poet Companion Journal (Print)

Everything is Writable: 240 Poetry Prompts from Two Sylvias Press
by Kelli Russell Agodon and Annette Spaulding-Convy (Print)

Fire On Her Tongue: An Anthology of Contemporary Women's Poetry
edited by Kelli Russell Agodon and Annette Spaulding-Convy (Print and eBook)

The Poet Tarot and Guidebook: A Deck Of Creative Exploration (Print)

The Inspired Poet: Writing Exercises to Spark New Work
by Susan Landgraf (Print)

The Whimsical Muse: Poetic Play for Busy Creatives
by Danell Jones (Print)

Shade of Blue Trees, Finalist 2019 Two Sylvias Press Wilder Prize
by Kelly Cressio-Moeller (Print)

Disappearing Queen, Winner of the 2019 Two Sylvias Press Wilder Prize
by Gail Martin (Print)

Deathbed Sext, Winner of the 2019 Two Sylvias Press Chapbook Prize
by Christopher Salerno (Print)

Crown of Wild, Winner of the 2018 Two Sylvias Press Wilder Prize
by Erica Bodwell (Print)

American Zero, Winner of the 2018 Two Sylvias Press Chapbook Prize
by Stella Wong (Print and eBook)

All Transparent Things Need Thundershirts, Winner of the 2017 Two Sylvias Press
Wilder Prize
by Dana Roeser (Print and eBook)

Where The Horse Takes Wing: The Uncollected Poems of Madeline DeFrees
edited by Anne McDuffie (Print and eBook)

In The House Of My Father, Winner of the 2017 Two Sylvias Press Chapbook Prize
by Hiwot Adilow (Print and eBook)

Box, Winner of the 2017 Two Sylvias Press Poetry Prize
by Sue D. Burton (Print and eBook)

Tsigan: The Gypsy Poem (New Edition)
by Cecilia Woloch (Print and eBook)

PR For Poets
by Jeannine Hall Gailey (Print and eBook)

Appalachians Run Amok, Winner of the 2016 Two Sylvias Press Wilder Prize
by Adrian Blevins (Print and eBook)

Pass It On!
by Gloria J. McEwen Burgess (Print)

Killing Marias
by Claudia Castro Luna (Print and eBook)

The Ego and the Empiricist, Finalist 2016 Two Sylvias Press Chapbook Prize
by Derek Mong (Print and eBook)

The Authenticity Experiment
by Kate Carroll de Gutes (Print and eBook)

Mytheria, Finalist 2015 Two Sylvias Press Wilder Prize
by Molly Tenenbaum (Print and eBook)

Arab in Newsland , Winner of the 2016 Two Sylvias Press Chapbook Prize
by Lena Khalaf Tuffaha (Print and eBook)

The Blue Black Wet of Wood, Winner of the 2015 Two Sylvias Press Wilder Prize
by Carmen R. Gillespie (Print and eBook)

Fire Girl: Essays on India, America, and the In-Between
by Sayantani Dasgupta (Print and eBook)

Blood Song
by Michael Schmeltzer (Print and eBook)

Naming The No-Name Woman,
Winner of the 2015 Two Sylvias Press Chapbook Prize
by Jasmine An (Print and eBook)

Community Chest
by Natalie Serber (Print)

Phantom Son: A Mother's Story of Surrender
by Sharon Estill Taylor (Print and eBook)

What The Truth Tastes Like
by Martha Silano (Print and eBook)

landscape/heartbreak
by Michelle Peñaloza (Print and eBook)

Earth, Winner of the 2014 Two Sylvias Press Chapbook Prize
by Cecilia Woloch (Print and eBook)

The Cardiologist's Daughter
by Natasha Kochicheril Moni (Print and eBook)

She Returns to the Floating World
by Jeannine Hall Gailey (Print and eBook)

Hourglass Museum
by Kelli Russell Agodon (eBook)

Cloud Pharmacy
by Susan Rich (eBook)

Dear Alzheimer's: A Caregiver's Diary & Poems
by Esther Altshul Helfgott (eBook)

Listening to Mozart: Poems of Alzheimer's
by Esther Altshul Helfgott (eBook)

Crab Creek Review 30th Anniversary Issue featuring Northwest Poets
edited by Kelli Russell Agodon and Annette Spaulding-Convy (eBook)

Please visit Two Sylvias Press (www.twosylviaspress.com) for information on purchasing our print books, eBooks, writing tools, and for submission guidelines for our annual book prizes.

The Wilder Series Poetry Book Prize

The Wilder Series Book Prize is an annual contest hosted by Two Sylvias Press. It is open to women over 50 years of age (established or emerging poets) and includes a $1000 prize, publication by Two Sylvias Press, 20 copies of the winning book, and a vintage, art nouveau pendant. Women submitting manuscripts may be poets with one or more previously published chapbooks/books or poets without any prior chapbook/book publications. The judges for the prize are Two Sylvias Press cofounders and coeditors, Kelli Russell Agodon and Annette Spaulding-Convy.

The Wilder Series Book Prize Winners and Finalists

2019:
Gail Martin, *Disappearing Queen* (Winner)
Kelly Cressio-Moeller, *Shade of Blue Trees* (Finalist)

2018:
Erica Bodwell, *Crown of Wild* (Winner)

2017:
Dana Roeser, *All Transparent Things Need Thundershirts* (Winner)

2016:
Adrian Blevins, *Appalachians Run Amok* (Winner)

2015:
Carmen R. Gillespie, *The Blue Black Wet of Wood* (Winner)
Molly Tenenbaum, *Mytheria* (Finalist)

Made in the USA
Middletown, DE
13 July 2021